Along the course of life, we must take the time to evaluate where we are.

The Blessed Place

Rest, Reflect, and be Renewed!

"Also I will ordain a place for my people Israel, and will plant them, and they shall be moved no more..." 1Chronicles 17:9a (KJV)

Tracey K. George

Copyright © 2015 Tracey K. George

All rights reserved. No part of this book may be reproduced or transmitted in any form or by any means, electronic or mechanical, including photocopying, recording, or by any information storage and retrieval system without permission in writing from the copyright owner except provided by United State of America copyright law.

Library of Congress Catalog Control Number: **2095253441**

ISBN-13: 978-0692379455
ISBN-10: 0692379452

Scripture quotations from the King James Version (KJV) of the Bible. Copyright © 1970 by Thomas Nelson, Inc.

Scripture quotations from Holman Christian Standard Bible (HCSB) copyright © 2003 by Holman Bible Publishers

Scripture quotations from The Message (MSG) copyright 2003 NavPress and Amplified Bible 1985 Zondervan Publishing House

Contents

Acknowledgements v

Introduction vii

Purpose 11

Process 17

Permanence 27

The Tools 32

About the Author 35

Coming Soon 37

Acknowledgements

> *I Chronicles 29:13 "Now therefore, our God, we give You thanks and praise Your glorious name." (HCSB)*

I would like to extend my sincere thanks to my, parents, Kenneth and Ruby George for all of their support and prayers.

To my children, Kenneth and Nitara thank you for being there.

To my assistant, Chandra, thank you for all the late nights of note taking and transcribing.

To Apostle William Dallas thank you for your encouraging words and keeping the fire lit!

To my 10th grade English teacher, Mrs. Clotilda Diggs thank you for encouraging me to keep writing.

To my editor Demetrica, thank you for your patience through this entire process. God did it!

To those I did not mention who have offered up prayers on my behalf, I thank you all!

Introduction

Have you ever longed for a calgon escape? I know I have! Noise Free...Drama Free...No Distractions...mmm! Sounds great doesn't it! Hold up one minute, before you rush off to locate a map to pinpoint the physical address to *'leave all your troubles behind boulevard'*...stop right where you are! Many of us over the course of our lives have considered a job, house, relationship, city, and state when thinking of where we are supposed to be especially when we feel stuck in our current situation. So let's fast forward a few months. You've got the new job, moved to the new city, and connected with new people. Now you feel like you are on top of the world. Celebration here you come. For those first few months, everything is great. What could possibly go wrong; you think. However, as time passes by, the excitement seems to wane; you don't feel the same. What happened? Can't quite put your finger on it? Did you make a mistake? You still feel empty. The honeymoon phase has ended. What went wrong? You continue to question everything. Even to the point of preparing for another move, job, or relationship and continuing the cycle until…. Whew, can we pause for a moment and take a nice long breath?

Agreed... let's breathe... In our day-to-day movement, do we stop long enough to consider the need to release and focus? God has so much for us. Unfortunately, we don't take the time necessary to gain knowledge from our life experiences...to transition. In other words, after the chaos or even the close of a chapter in your life, it is necessary to take a break or a moment of silence. Yes! We're in such a hurry that we miss the quiet opportunities to rest, reflect, and to be renewed. In some cases, we have allowed our desire for the instant and quick to keep us from resting in the place He has designed. As a result, we wander around aimlessly or refuse to leave that one spot we've been in for years. Let me interject right here...Folks don't miss your moment because you feel it must happen right now. I'm not talking about the opportunity to advance materialistically. No, I'm talking about an intimate relationship with God, the time spent in the quiet place away from the humdrum of everyday issues. What we fail to realize is a real bond with God takes time to develop; yet it is essential for our development spiritually, mentally, etc... Too many relationships, families, ministries, and businesses have been destroyed because someone failed to humble themselves, slow down, and allow the time needed to evolve. We must be willing to submit ourselves to Him so we will know His will for our lives...the place He ordained for us. Now some would say they're doing just fine, while others would sum it up a bit differently. I believe this is a good spot for a moment of reflection and the acknowledgment of a place we've been avoiding. Is it possible we didn't know this place existed or didn't bother to question its existence? What were God's intentions concerning His children? What did He say about the components of the blessed place or the makeup of it? How is it designed? What did He intend for this place to be? When He said come and let us reason together... What did He have in mind? It is in this place that He wants to meet us. The place many overlooked or took for granted. He knows without proper care and guidance we would easily burn out...consequently, many have.

>Isaiah 1:18 (KJV)
>
>*"Come now, and let us reason together, saith the Lord: though your sins be as scarlet, they shall be as white as snow; though they be red like crimson, they shall be as wool." (Emphasis added)*

Is it possible? Is there a "place" that we can be both safe and secure? Is there a place where we can hear from our Father and feel strength as we walk through our journey of life? With God's continued guidance, it's a no brainer!

How would it feel to know that God has ordered your steps? If you haven't taken the time to comprehend it, when will you? Or do we continually meander through life not paying any attention to the importance of the place we are in and did God want us there. For Job, it was the eye in the middle of the storm. Where is that place for you? For me? How many of us have ever considered that God already has the information we need and it would be easier tuning in to Him?

The steps of a good man are ORDERED by the Lord... So...what are we doing to ourselves? Have we forgotten that God knows everything? So what did He say? Did we even bother to ask Him for His direction for our lives? How did we get to the place of making our own decisions without firm guidance from the Lord? Trust me, He knows and is patient enough to watch as we mess it up. Then with a still small voice, if we let Him, He will show us where we missed it and help us to our BLESSED PLACE! It begins...

Purpose

Proverbs 18:10 (MSG) "God's name is a place of protection—good people can run there and be safe."

Acknowledging God is a key component of the blessed place. In fact, it is crucial. Do we recognize God's authority? Do we give Him the honor due His name? Do we reverence him? Our lives should reflect that. The Blessed Place offers us the opportunity to stop and recognize Him as the King. Nothing else matters or makes sense without this information being at the forefront of our mind. Psalms 47:7 tells us that God is the King of all the earth: sing ye praises with understanding.

Folks, there we have it...understanding. We need to be aware. Wandering aimlessly through life when information is available is foolish. He told us in his word:

> Proverbs 4:7 (KJV)
>
> "Wisdom is the principal thing; therefore get wisdom: and with all thy getting, get understanding."

The journey through life with no awareness, perception, appreciation, etc. will eventually lead to frustration, bitterness, and even stagnancy. Hence, the reason we must allow ourselves to embrace the blessed place...its existence!

The "Aha" moment is realizing that there is such a place for us. God has us in mind. Wow! Can you grasp the fact that God
sanctioned for us to be in a place that He authorized for us to dwell. A place of intimacy with Him.

A place deemed necessary for steady growth and maturity. There's something to be said when we are in the place, the moment, the stance that God wants for us at the time He wants it. Do we miss it at times? Yes we do! That's why we must know his intent.

The blessed place is a state of mind and yet the time/season where God puts our life on pause so we can be given direction away from all the distractions. He did this for Elijah after running from Jezebel to a cave. For Moses after he fled to Midian once the news of murdering the Egyptian had spread. Where has He led you, prior to the next point in your life? Did you skip that part?

The substratum of the blessed place is obedience. When you learn that there is safety in obeying God then you're in position to move out of God's way as He directs your path. The Spirit led Jesus into the wilderness. When you are obedient to His instructions for your life, you welcome the opportunities to learn, develop, grow, and mature. These lessons come through life experiences, tragedies, issues, etc. He leads us through the valley of the shadow of death. Yet we do not have to fear any evil. Why? God is walking with us.

Realizing that fact, changes everything. It takes into consideration the time, season, and stance of our life. The Blessed Place affords us the ability to develop and maintain a real relationship with God while we are here on earth.

Do you find yourself in a valley of decision trying to figure out your entire life? The location, the appointment, and our position are shown to us once we take the time to rest in Him. After everything we've been through, we need this time! Where is the place we can occupy right now that allows focus and the opportunity to remain centered no matter what's going on? It is the Blessed Place. Could this be one of the reasons we were told to take on the mind of Christ? Hmm!

God knew we needed His support and protection. He also knew we needed guidance on how to get the help. Unfortunately, many of us have a hard time admitting we need assistance. Greater still, we have to face the fact that change can be unsettling at times and truthfully some would prefer for things to remain the same. Yet we pray for God to do this or that and He watches us struggle through the process of transitioning from where we are to where we need to be. How well do I remember signing on the dotted line to become a soldier? Picture if you will a scrawny kid with big eyes yet a word from the Lord that led me to what I considered at the time to be a God-forsaken place.

Really...what was I thinking? Tracey George a soldier? So there I was, at the ripe age of nineteen, on my way to New

Jersey to begin Basic Training. Help Lord! I arrived at Fort Dix, New Jersey full of excitement, anticipation, and a heavy dose of nervousness. The first few days were a rude awakening; not one for quitting, I decided to make the best of it and learn all I could. While engaging in the routine pushups and other forms of rigorous training to the constant yelling overheard from the Drill Sergeants, I questioned my decision to join the United States Army Reserves. We followed a rigid schedule...I mean it was gruesome! Waking up 3:30 in the morning while the sun was still asleep...then enter the mess hall (cafeteria) only to eat so fast you don't remember what it was, classes every day, physical exercises that challenged every muscle in your body to go above and beyond. It was demanding yet needed. I didn't see the connection between basic and becoming a soldier. Believe me, I wasn't the only one complaining. At the end of training, we marched in front of the officials of BT (Basic Training) with our heads held high. We kept the faith and finished our course. So, now it was official, we were soldiers. The road to becoming what I signed up for was treacherous but needed in the changeover.

  Just like my time in basic training, our Father knew that we need the discipline to stay grounded. On our own, we would wander from place to place. An idle mind is open for every distraction under the sun. We tend to get into trouble when we attempt to go through life without His direction and support.

When we come to God, we are like a diamond in the raw; He knows we still carry baggage from yesteryear and need help with unloading. In addition, we have no knowledge of the true meaning of what it is to walk with Him. Sure, some of us have learned how to "do church" yet lack a real appreciation of what it means to develop our relationship with the One who brought us in. Over time, there is an inclination to become complacent with what we see around us without considering that there is so much more.

Many have a hard time understanding what happens after you leave one phase of life and move into the next. There's a time of transition, an interruption in the journey. Identifying this is most important in freeing yourself from the old wine skins, appreciating life lessons, allowing the joy of the morning, and the beauty of sweet release from all the clutter experienced in the previous chapters of life.

Maturity is an important part of life and essential; nevertheless, without learning life lessons how can we get there. Whether we lack rest or we haven't learned something necessary for our next step, He designed for there to be different levels of pause in our life. From a moment of reflection to a time of absolute stillness, He knows what it would take to get us going or redirect us when we are off course.

Psalms 46:10 (KJV)

"Be still, and know that I am God: I will be exalted among the heathen, I will be exalted in the earth."

In your blessed place, you learn to stop and appreciate the life lessons. If we are honest, we prefer the good times, the great relationships, the magnificent job opportunities, etc... there's nothing wrong with that! I prefer them too. However, what do you do when all hell is breaking loose? While you're enjoying everything time didn't stand still, instead more was added to the plate. Issues became magnified beyond compare. Every situation grew; on the job, the family, and everywhere else. Whew! The honey in the moon has turned to drama at every single turn.

Have you developed your relationship to the point of knowing what to do and who to turn to when that season of drama comes? Do you know how to seek God for instructions? Remember what God does is help us journey through when those amazing things don't feel so amazing. He guides us away from the interruptions as we learn to face forward through every trial. With the right information, it encourages us to process through and grow instead of running away in a position of avoidance. We are reminded of the order, the instructions, and the need to sit still.

Process

Psalms 119:1-5 (MSG)

"You're blessed when you stay on course, walking steadily on the road revealed by God. You're blessed when you follow his directions, doing your best to find him. That's right—you don't go off on your own; you walk straight along the road he set. You, God, prescribed the right way to live; now you expect us to live it."

What course are you on? How do you stay on course when you don't know what it is? I'm glad you asked. We do not have to wander around aimlessly without direction. We can have support along the way.

With everything going on in life all the problems, trials, drama, etc...etc...etc... on the flip side, things were fine then out of the blue...so much! How do you get through it all? The easiest thing to do...Avoid everything! Run as fast as you can to the nearest exit and leave. Does this sound like a plan? No! This is precisely what some do when the going gets tough. What would you do if you knew you weren't alone and there was a method to the madness?

Proverbs 14:8 (MSG)

*"The wisdom of the wise keeps life on track;
the foolishness of fools lands them in the ditch."*

In the course of life, whether you realize it or not there is a process... (A series of actions that produce something or lead to a particular result). While sitting in the pool of frustration over whatever you find yourself in at the moment have you considered the procedure? I know... in the middle of it all, the last thing on your mind is "Gee" I need to process through this or that. Seriously, we must get to the place of understanding the need to allow development. The method by which God plans to transition us from point A to point B, the key to relieving ourselves from all the unnecessary stress and tension; in other words, the process.

Drifting around through life with no real direction or course of action is unwise. Can you say I am tired of being sick due to constant worry and anxiety?

God had us in mind not just to create us. He took into consideration that we would need time and space for development as we live out this thing called life. Let that soak in for a minute...how amazing! In Psalms, He told us:

> Psalms 119:1-8 (MSG)
>
> *"You're blessed when you stay on course, walking steadily on the road revealed by GOD. You're blessed when you follow his directions, doing your best to find him. That's right—you don't go off on your own; you walk straight along the road he set. You, GOD, prescribed the right way to live; now you expect us to live it. Oh, that my steps might be steady, keeping to the course you set; then I'd never have any regrets in comparing my life with your counsel. I thank you for speaking straight from your heart; I learn the pattern of your righteous*

> *ways. I'm going to do what you tell me to do, don't ever walk off, and leave me."*

We enter the blessed place whenever adjustments need to be made. If we refuse to go to that quiet place when He beckons then we will have some repercussions. It's necessary to regroup, to rest, to be renewed...To reorganize...For deposit. Along the course of life we must reconsider where we are. Through honest observation concerning life issues, decisions, and goals, we should stop and have another look at self. Are you on target? Are you where God placed you? Have you grown or matured? Did you lose focus along the way?

It's okay...really, it is. We must take the time to ask ourselves the hard questions to get a clear perspective of where we are. In fact, take some time and think about it right now. Be honest with yourself. Real self-assessment gives the opportunity for reflection. Without the hindrances, we are able to recognize some of the things that has limited or prevented our progression. After some reflection where are you?

Many are in the valley of decisions (Joel 3:14). What crossroad do you find yourself on? Roughing it through the years moving between jobs and relationships without pause, did you consider the necessity for transition? Perhaps you felt you were strong enough to handle the buildup of stress on top of stress. Without a break or retreat, eventually, your body will shut down. At the point of burnout is a sign that you were long overdue for the time to regroup.

I know we can be hardheaded and downright stubborn when it comes to getting what we want when we want it. Yes, I admit, I have been a bit impatient at times, too eager to get on with life. Why should I have to wait? I have been faithful and studied the word. You know the list we repeat when we feel slighted in the least. I figured God would want me to move on to the next phase and became frustrated when the opposite would happen. Instead of moving expeditiously, I was placed on pause. Certain opportunities would show up and I had to say no. At first, I felt forsaken by my Father; as time passed I came to the conclusion that I had more growing to do and He didn't want any of the old baggage (yesterday's way of thinking) to impede my progress. It was time for a brief break to appreciate the previous season of my life and to acknowledge God's presence regardless of the pressures I faced. Years ago, I thought that time would heal all wounds (a familiar phrase I'm sure you remember hearing). However, I discovered through God's guidance that time without training, forgiveness, reflection, appreciation, admittance to your own craziness is just time. Let me emphasize that...Time devoid of guidance in His word gets old real quick. Years later, the lack of necessary changes will eventually reveal someone who is immature and possibly bitter with many chips on their shoulders expecting everybody to feel sorry for them because of how life has been.

Well, okay…You suffered a major setback or perhaps a traumatic experience, which calls for you to take the time to weep, be silent, or pinpoint some things. Seriously, did life get the best of you? Were the storms too much to handle? Sure, we've all had difficulties that hit us from so many different angles that we wanted to scream. Does that sound familiar to you? When you dedicated your life to the Lord, did you really consider the cost? Were you increasing in wisdom? Were you experiencing a journey with God that superseded every other relationship in your life while fueling those very relationships to excel? If we were honest, most of us were too excited and overwhelmed with glee from "the new"; we really did not understand the depth of what was taking place.

With everything going on, in this voyage of life, who stops long enough to consider instructions, peace, and rest? Nevertheless, we need to keep in mind the proper procedure for this road to be traveled. What are the perimeters? What is the tone? Are there adjustments that need to be made? Have you become a wanderer? What are we supposed to bring to the table? We now have an opportunity to stand still.

Psalms 19:7-8 (KJV)

"The instruction of the Lord is perfect,
renewing one's life;
the testimony of the Lord is trustworthy,
making the inexperienced wise.
8 The precepts of the Lord are right,
making the heart glad;

> the command of the Lord is radiant,
> making the eyes light up."

Too often, we find ourselves wandering around with no real clue of His directives. Sure life goes on. We know that things happen. Sometimes we receive curve balls in life without warning or memo. Yet God has orchestrated for us a place in Him that will assist us with weathering life storms.

> Psalm 119:105, 114 (AMP)
>
> "Your word is a lamp to my feet and a light to my path. [Prov. 6:23.] You are my hiding place and my shield; I hope in Your word. "[Ps. 32:7; 91:1.]

Let me put it like this...When I went to BT (basic training), everything was ready and waiting for our arrival. We had to follow the instructions of utter strangers as they instilled in us the army values. We signed up to be soldiers and the rest was up to them. There was a process. We learned so much about the code of conduct, teamwork, discipline, and more. They trained us to think, eat, and sleep, like a soldier; but the title of soldier wasn't given until we completed the assignment of basic training.

Do you hold a position yet do not walk in the statutes that go along with it? Do you find yourself carrying a title, acquiring honor, sitting in the seat, yet have little to no understanding of what you possess? Or do you hold a position for which you have shown little to no regard for.

When we are open to Him, God gives us the needed information to move forward with alertness... focused and determined. Failure to follow His instructions can adversely hamper or prohibit our ability to mature. We must allow change to occur. God trims/prunes us so we can produce more fruit and remain connected to the True Vine. Prepare for correction. Yes, I said it! Here goes another reality check. If your
walk with God is going to be a successful one then you have to approach Him in the manner that He said. He expects us to come to Him as dear children. Now on paper that sounds fine, but how many adults are willing to throw away their grown cards in favor of a sandbox? For many this part of the kingdom mindset is hard. Yet God knows we need it. If you want His attention then rethink your approach. If you want the Instructor then approach as a student. If you want the attention of the Father, approach as a child.

> Mark 10:15 (AMP)
>
> *"Truly I tell you, whoever does not receive and accept and welcome the kingdom of God like a little child [does] positively shall not enter it at all."*

Coming to the Father in a childlike manner means there will be times of correction. He is aware of the problem as well as how we got trapped in it. He understands that without His pruning we will continue to go through life with all this dead weight and old stuff. God chastens those He loves. This means we will be chastised from time to time. Why? He loves us!

Psalms 23:1-6 (MSG)

> "God, my shepherd! I don't need a thing. You have bedded me down in lush meadows; you find me quiet pools to drink from. True to your word, you let me catch my breath and send me in the right direction. Even when the way goes through Death Valley, I'm not afraid when you walk at my side. Your trusty shepherd's crook makes me feel secure. You serve me a six-course dinner right in front of my enemies. You revive my drooping head; my cup brims with blessing. Your beauty and love chase after me every day of my life. I'm back home in the house of God for the rest of my life."

There are times when we feel slighted because an unexpected halt triggered a shift or change to our well-constructed plans. Continually frustrated by the abrupt interruptions, we have a tendency to make hasty decisions that could potentially cause damage to other areas of our life.

Proverbs 19:21 (MSG)

> "We humans keep brainstorming options and plans, but God's purpose prevails."

Remember during your life there's a real need to rest, reflect, and be renewed. Whether due to the loss of employment, the termination of a relationship, or some other form of traumatic experience having a solid connection with God affords you the moment to be still and know. Even if all seems peachy-keen, we still need the blessed place to exist in our lives! Knowing that I am not on this journey alone has been the key to my own sanity. It is refreshing to continue through life with information received from life lessons.

So, if it is a time of training for you and you skip ahead to do something else or if it is a season of rest and you are still hard at it then you will miss your opportunity to grasp vital information that has the potential to catapult your life into the next phase.

No more excuses...No more lingering behind refusing to go/remain in the blessed place. In this day and time, it has become easy to use the excuse "I'm only human". Let's face it we need to raise our expectations. What did God say? Have falling and failure become a way of life or have we learned to accept mediocrity? We must consider the alarming fact that continuing to make excuses causes one to believe that the standard that God set is impossible for anyone to achieve. At some point, we began to measure ourselves by other people and based on the outcome we decide whether we are on point or not. In actuality, we have set ourselves up to lower our standards so that we don't expect much from our own lives. Staying on course reminds us that there is a goal and I'm not out here just wandering around with no focus, no direction, etc.

This means we all have work to do. We have to take the time to dust off and assess the damage. For example, after a fall, many assume all I have to do is get up and keep going. That is not true. A real assessment is needed for a proper diagnosis of what happened and the nature of the injury. As a kid, some may remember falling down or tripping while playing with friends. I did. For some they cried and were consoled by their peers and eventually returned to play. While others needed a little more than a pat on the back and quick shoulder-rub by a buddy. For those who required more, they went home to mom or an older person who provided TLC, Band-Aids, ointment, and words of comfort. In other words, some setbacks require more than a quick it's all good response.

Isaiah 52:2(KJV)

Shake thyself from the dust; ARISE, and SIT DOWN, Jerusalem: loose thyself from the bands of thy neck, O captive daughter of Zion.

Permanence

John 15:4 (KJV)
"Abide in me, and I in you. As the branch cannot bear fruit of itself, except it abide in the vine; no more can ye, except ye abide in me."

Sometimes we wonder where we are going and will we ever get there. Other times we feel as if we are there and then realize; that ain't it! You know you're in your blessed place when you are at peace regardless of the circumstances, storms, and issues.

The place of tranquility and renewal is a part of that place. You are in the palm of God's hand and you know it! You are focused and alert. What is this? It is your Blessed Place.

Psalm 27:4-6 (MSG)

"I'm asking God for one thing, only one thing: To live with him in his house my whole life long. I'll contemplate his beauty; I'll study at his feet. That's the only quiet, secure place in a noisy world, the perfect getaway, far from the buzz of traffic. God holds me head and shoulders above all who try to pull me down. I'm headed for his place to offer anthems that will raise the roof! Already I'm singing God-songs; I'm making music to God."

One thing...only one thing did the writer desire. The writer shares with us his one desire to live with God in His house for the duration of his life. He asked God could he live with Him NOW. Wow! What a privilege and honor to be able to live this way, contemplating His beauty, far from the noise and distractions that so easily beset us. Learning life lessons at His feet on a continual basis is a part of the Blessed Place.

Throughout our journey storms approach and even attempt to overtake yet knowing that God is in control brings a sense of awareness that He really has you in the palm of His hand.

> Psalm 119:1a (MSG)
>
> "You're blessed when you stay on course, walking steadily on the road revealed by God!"

Something else to consider on our journey is the season and time in life where some may stay in our lives while others have to leave. To put it mildly, we tend to put blinders on when dealing with others i.e. friends, family, business partners, etc. As we learn more about ourselves, we discover what is needed in our life. Unfortunately, we tend to be a society that takes family and friends with us, regardless of their behavior, integrity, and the overall picture.

We make sure those special ones aren't left out. He may not be the right one for the job, BUT he's your brother. She may have a bad attitude yet we will place her in a job working directly with people because we grew up together. The list is endless yet we have our reasons for bending the rules in favor of our kin.

When God is ready to do something in your life sometimes, we fail to consider the ins and outs. Perhaps you are right where you need to be or on your way there. Yet there is a problem. God has given you a sign of some type letting you know that it is time to move forward.

He may have shown you that He has more for you and it is time to take the plunge. However, you decide to take some folks with you.

> Psalm 15:1-3 (KJV)
>
> "Lord, who shall abide in thy tabernacle? Who shall dwell in thy holy hill? ^{2} He that walketh uprightly, and worketh righteousness, and speaketh the truth in his heart ^{3} He that backbiteth not with his tongue, nor doeth evil to his neighbour, nor taketh up a reproach against his neighbour."

Are you the one that others tend to lean on for whatever reason so naturally you figured that it would be okay to bring some along for the ride? Have you considered the fact that it isn't their time? Maybe they don't desire to go any further but are willing to tag along even if it means getting in the way.

Now when you received the directives from God, He was specific. He told you to go. So what happened that caused the assumption that others could go? Yes, I know, we try to be nice. We want to see others make it.

Did we ever consider the fact that they may not be ready or that God wanted you to go alone? Unfortunately, we fail to realize in these cases that God's ways and thoughts are higher than ours, as shown to us in Judges 1:1-3.

> Judges 1: 1-3 (MSG)
>
> "1 A time came after the death of Joshua when the People of Israel asked GOD, "Who will take the lead in going up against the Canaanites to fight them?"
>
> 2 And GOD said, "Judah will go. I've given the land to him."
>
> 3 The men of Judah said to those of their brother Simeon, "Go up with us to our territory and we'll fight the Canaanites. Then we'll go with you to your territory." And Simeon went with them."

The people of Israel asked God, who will take the lead and He said Judah! He did not say any other names beside that. Yet after He spoke, the men of Judah went and asked Simeon if they would go with them. Really? Can we be honest?

Oftentimes, we hear God clearly say one thing and then we run off and do something totally different. Then we are left wondering why it didn't work as we "planned."

How hard is it to remember that in God's kingdom, He is in charge! There are times, I know, God will send you to live, work, or minister in a place yet you have no desire to be there. Or perhaps, you desire to remain angry over an issue that God has called you to be at peace with. In your relationship with Him, He is the director and we are to follow His lead. He knows and sees what we have closed our eyes and ears to.

Realizing that the season for that person or that assignment has ended is the key to your own growth. Let them move on. Thank God for the time that they were in your life. The impact was necessary. Have no regrets. Some may say they dumped me. However, it does not matter. Thank them for the time and move on.

The real issue is for them to leave and then years later, you find yourself same spot frustrated and bitter. No more, Run now to your blessed place and allow God to bring comfort to your tired soul!

The Tools

After learning about the blessed place and the whole point of it all, it's time to check in and actually put it to work in your own life. Go to our Father with an open mind and a willing heart. No pretense here. Admit your stuff. Lay it all at His feet then sit still so He can speak to you. In this moment of pause, He'll give you directives for your life. You'll learn the road to take, the season you're in, and what you'll be expected to do while there. This place requires a change in mindset and obedience to God's voice. Be open to the realization that this is your process.

How do I stay in the blessed place when everything around me seems chaotic? Are you ready to develop and maintain permanence in the Blessed Place?

> *Psalm 91:1-4, 9 (AMP)*
>
> *HE WHO dwells in the secret place of the Most High shall remain stable and fixed under the shadow of the Almighty [Whose power no foe can withstand]. I will say of the Lord, He is my Refuge and my Fortress, my God; on Him, I lean and rely, and in Him I [confidently] trust! For [then] He will deliver you from the snare of the fowler and from the deadly pestilence. [Then] He will cover you with His pinions, and under His wings shall you trust and find refuge; His truth and His faithfulness are a shield and a buckler. ^{9} Because you have made the Lord your refuge, and the Most High your dwelling place," [Ps. 91:1, 14.]*

Are you prepared for this to become your way of life and not a temporary fix? Are you willing to walk in His will as He gets the glory out of your life? Let go of everything and everyone hindering you from moving forward. All the dead weight!

Hang onto every life lesson learned. Yes, keep those! Those lessons assist you as you move forward in your life journey. Re-align yourself with those who have the same mindset. Recognize the importance of staying where God planted you. You know you are there when everything around you is stormy yet you are focused.

Even cars need a moment to be refueled or a period of time to be repaired. We seem to think we can keep moving from place to place, situation to situation, and issue to issue without a moment of pause. Hence, the reason so many end-up drained, burned out, having a series of panic attacks, nervous breakdowns, or their body completely shuts down. This happens because we forget to Selah (pause and think). Some moments require a few seconds or a minute or two while others require a leave of absence. The Blessed Place; He hides you while you reflect, regroup, and recharge. It is time to prepare for your pause. Here you are no longer a wanderer, you are on the right path! You are safe and secure. This is God's perfect will for your life!

Welcome you are now in your Blessed Place!

About the Author

Tracey George, B.S. in Psychology, is the Overseer of The Core Training Institute, The Core Outreach Network, and a Certified Life Transitions and Leadership Coach with TGAP Consultants. She has written for two anthologies 'This Far by Faith' edited by Vanessa Miller, 'Dear Daddy' edited by Angela Smith, and blogs for the Women to Women (W.O.W) organization of which she is a member.

Tracey lives with her family in South Carolina. She has been blessed to travel throughout the U.S. and overseas ministering the gospel through word and song.
She speaks regularly to singles, married couples, church congregations, ministerial leaders, business staff, and management about resolving conflict issues.
To learn more about her or the ministries mentioned feel free to visit her on the web at www.thetgap.com or email her at katrinage.tg@gmail.com

Do you desire to get moving with your life especially after a stormy situation?
Are you at a point in your life where some readjustments need to be made?
Do you have questions concerning your destiny and/or purpose in life?
Then this is a* GRAND OPPORTUNITY *tailored made just for you!

FREE INTRODUCTORY SESSION
with
Certified Life Transitions and Leadership Coach
Tracey K. George

TAKE FULL ADVANTAGE OF THIS FREE INTRODUCTORY OFFER AND LET ME HELP YOU ON YOUR WAY!

Coming Soon

Touch the World-CD

Tracey 'KatrinaGe' George

www.reverbnation.com/katrinage
www.thetgap.com

www.ingramcontent.com/pod-product-compliance
Lightning Source LLC
Chambersburg PA
CBHW061314040426
42444CB00010B/2628